You Are Stardust

Stardust

Elin Kelsey

Artwork by Soyeon Kim

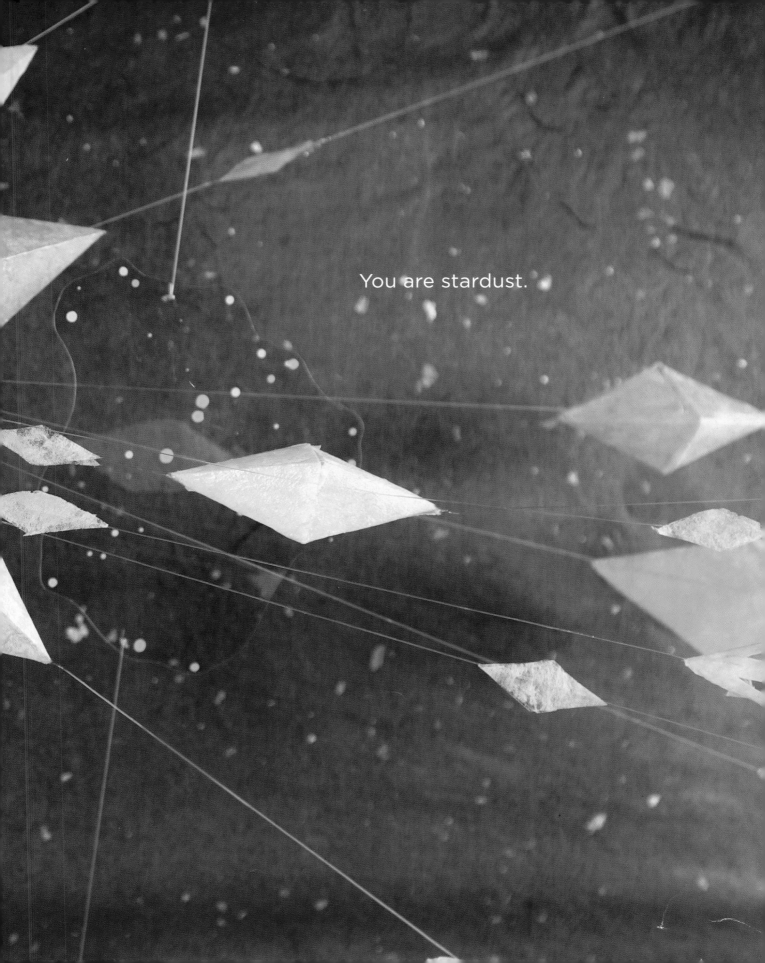

You are stardust.

Every tiny atom in your body came from a star that exploded long before you were born.

You started life as a single cell.
So did all other creatures on planet Earth.

Like fish deep in the ocean,
you called salt water home.
You swam inside the salty sea
of your mother's womb.

Salt still flows through your veins, your sweat and your tears. The sea within you is as salty as the ocean.

The water swirling in your glass once filled the puddles where dinosaurs drank.

From ocean to sky to land and back again, the same water has been quenching thirsts for millions of years.

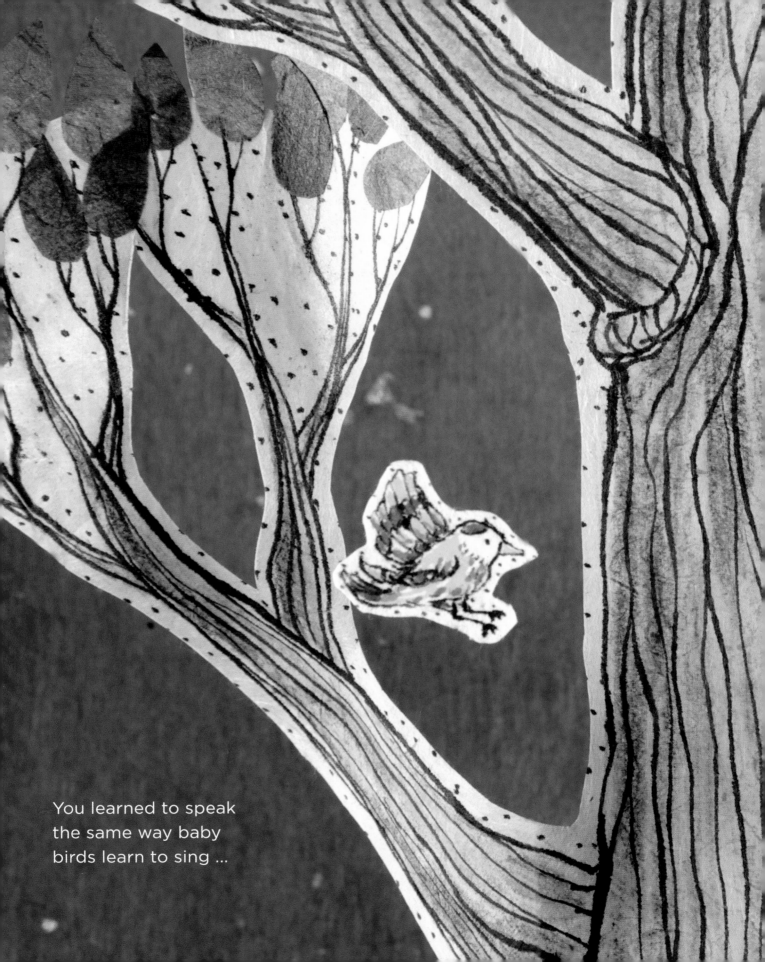

You learned to speak
the same way baby
birds learn to sing ...

... by chatting with your parents.
"Ma ma ma!"
"Tweet tweet tweet!"

Be still.
Listen.

Like you, the
Earth breathes.

Your breath is alive with the promise of flowers.

Each time you blow a kiss to the world, you spread pollen that might grow to be a new plant.

Inside your brain, electricity
stronger than lightning
powers your every thought.

You sneeze with the force of a tornado.
Wind rockets from your nose quicker
than a cheetah sprints.

You grow at night
when your bones are resting,
just like the sheep you count
to help you sleep.

You may sprout even taller
in the spring and summer, just
like the plants in your garden.

Your hair falls like
autumn leaves.

You tend to shed the most hair in early autumn and save your thickest growth for the heart of winter.

Your body constantly changes.

New cells line your stomach
every three days.

You'll replace your skin
100 times by the time you
turn 10.

Just as forests grow new trees
in place of old ones ...

... you grow entirely new
skeletons throughout
your life.

If you were a planet, you'd be a lot like the Earth.

Rainforests on land and algae in the oceans are the Earth's lungs.

From your head to your toes,
inside and out, billions of teeny
micro-organisms live on planet You.

You know how it feels to be a good friend and so do other animals.

Bats and sperm whales get their friends to babysit.

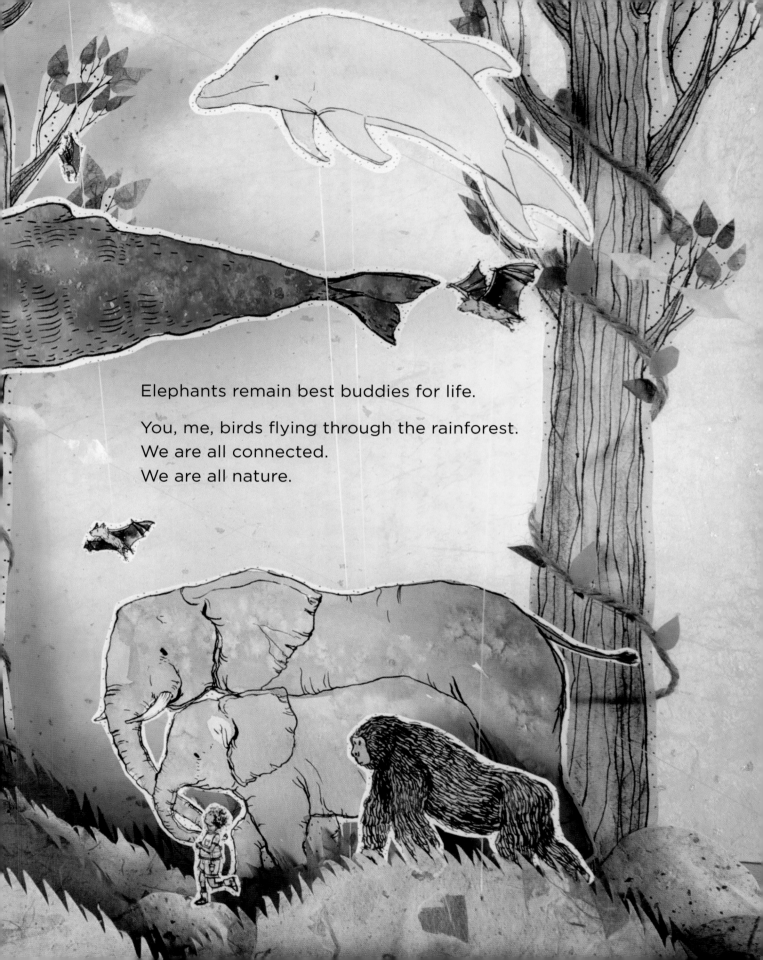

Elephants remain best buddies for life.

You, me, birds flying through the rainforest.
We are all connected.
We are all nature.

We are all stardust.